BROTHERS IN ARMS

A True World War II Story of Wojtek the Bear
and the Soldiers Who Loved Him

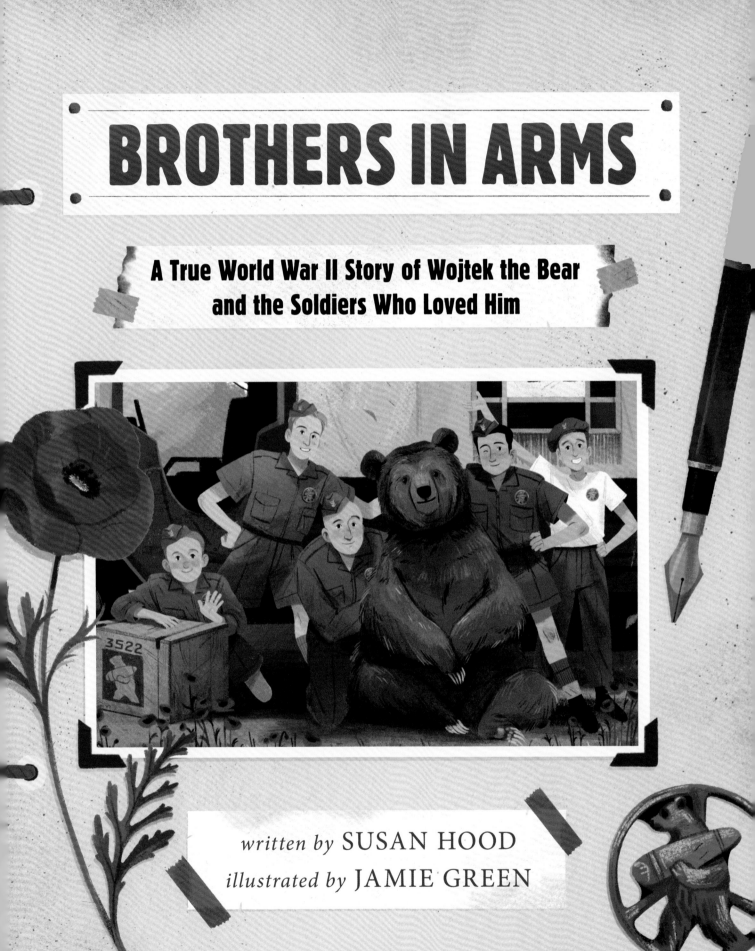

written by SUSAN HOOD
illustrated by JAMIE GREEN

HARPER
An Imprint of HarperCollinsPublishers

AUTHOR'S NOTE

During World War II, two fierce armies—Hitler's German Nazis and Stalin's Soviet soldiers—invaded Poland and cut the country in half. The Soviets rounded up at least 1.25 million Polish people and sent them to slave labor camps in Siberia.

Two years later, Hitler attacked his former friends, the Soviets. Stalin responded by releasing his Polish prisoners of war if they would fight Hitler in the newly formed Anders' Army, commanded by General Władysław Anders.

Thousands of men and women, accompanied by children, streamed south on foot, freight trains, filthy wagons, and ferries to Allied army training camps in the Middle East.

It was in Iran (then called Persia) that some of these evacuees met a little boy holding a mysterious sack. That was the start of the true story of an orphaned bear cub and how he traveled from that boy to a young woman to a general and finally to his new family, his brothers in arms.

For Sophie & Molly & bear lovers everywhere!—*S.H.*

To Mom, Dad, and our shy little Wojtek, Suki —*J.G.*

Brothers in Arms: A True World War II Story of Wojtek the Bear and the Soldiers Who Loved Him • Text copyright © 2022 by Susan Hood • Illustrations copyright © 2022 by Jamie Green • All rights reserved. Manufactured in Italy. • No part of this book may be used or reproduced in any manner whatsoever without written permission except in the case of brief quotations embodied in critical articles and reviews. For information address HarperCollins Children's Books, a division of HarperCollins Publishers, 195 Broadway, New York, NY 10007. www.harpercollinschildrens.com • Library of Congress Control Number: 2021946935 • ISBN 978-0-06-306476-8 • The artist used Procreate to create the digital illustrations for this book • Typography by Caitlin Stamper
22 23 24 25 26 RTLO 10 9 8 7 6 5 4 3 2 1 ❖ First Edition

How to pronounce the names in this book:

Wojtek—*VOY-tek*

Irena Bokiewicz—*EE-rena Bo-KAY-vitch*

Wojciech Narębski—*VOY-cheh Na-REB-ski*
Note: Wojtek is a nickname for Wojciech.

Piotr Prendyś—*PYOTR (or Peter) PRAN-dis*

Henryk Zacharewicz—*Hen-RY-ka Za-ha-RE-vitsch*

Dymitr Szawlugo—*Di-MI-tree Shav-LU-go*

General Władysław Anders—*VLA-dis-waff*

APRIL 8, 1942

The cherry blossoms were in bloom when a young woman named Irena, her mother, and a caravan of bedraggled travelers met a young boy in the mountains of Persia. He was holding a sack. Look! Something was moving inside. Irena and her friends peered into the bag. Big brown eyes stared back at them . . .

It was a bear! People crowded around to gape at the tiny orphan. He was so cuddly, so helpless. He filled them with warmth, rekindling feelings of tenderness the labor camps had nearly snuffed out. Irena was enchanted by the little cub. A lieutenant handed the boy a few coins to buy him for her.

Delighted, Irena scooped the bear up. Here was someone to love. Someone who would love her. She would be his mother now.

Irena brought her baby to the civilian camp near Tehran. But the rambunctious bear kept the others awake at night. He was a pain in the neck!

He rose early and stole their breakfasts, eating the eggs and throwing the rest on the ground. Heartsick, Irena realized this Syrian brown bear would soon grow to be five hundred pounds. Get rid of him, everyone cried. But she couldn't just abandon him.

AUGUST 1942

Irena met a visiting general and saw how his soldiers were smitten with the irresistible orphan. After all, many of them were orphans, too. When Stalin and Hitler invaded Poland, the soldiers had lost their families, their homes, their country. Marching south, they were all bone-tired and war-weary, but the cub made them laugh. He was an instant morale builder!

The general agreed to adopt the bear; Irena was grateful to find her friend a good home. The troops named the bear Wojtek (*VOY-tek*), short for a Polish name that means "happy warrior."

When the troops marched on, the bear marched too. He stood on his hind legs and, to the amusement of the soldiers, walked just as they did.

When they rode in jeeps, the soldiers grinned as bystanders gasped in astonishment at the furry fellow in the passenger seat.

The soldiers and their new mascot traveled to a large Allied training camp in Gedera, near the Mediterranean Sea. There they joined forces with other soldiers. Together, these men would become Wojtek's new family.

SEPTEMBER 1942

In camp, Wojtek slept in a tent just as the men did. He had his own bed, but he often preferred the warmth and comfort of crawling into bed with tentmate Lance Corporal Piotr (Peter) Prendyś.

"The bear treated [Peter] as a father," said soldier Wojciech, the longest surviving member of the company. Some of the men teased Peter, calling him Mother Bear. Peter, who had been separated from his wife and children in the war, just smiled wistfully. He'd pull little Wojtek up on his lap whenever the cub needed a cuddle. Peter wouldn't admit it, but he seemed to need comforting as much as the bear did.

Any time was mealtime for Wojtek. He ate army rations, just as the men did. His friends indulged his sweet tooth, feeding him fruit, marmalade, honey, and syrup.

When the soldiers threw oranges in grenade practice, Wojtek cleaned up.
Takeout from the cookhouse was Wojtek's favorite fast food.
With his insatiable appetite, Wojtek grew . . .

and grew . . .

and grew.

Two teenage soldiers named Henryk and Dymitr became the growing bear's closest friends. Both boys were small and agile. They loved to play, box, and wrestle with Wojtek, as they had with their friends back home.

They pulled each other down and rolled over and over on the ground. The soldiers' uniforms got muddy and torn, but the men were never harmed. If Wojtek managed to pin his opponent, he would lick him in the face. "Even though he was in a bear skin," said soldier Wojciech, "we used to say he has a Polish soul. He was very kind . . . very sociable. He felt as if he were one of the gang."

The gang included a four-legged friend—a dalmatian named Kirkuk. When the two first met, Wojtek stared at Kirkuk's tail wagging back and forth, back and forth. Suddenly Kirkuk dashed off and Wojtek scampered after him! When Kirkuk's tail was just within reach, the clever dog skidded to a stop and the cub somersaulted over him. This became a favorite game, and soon the two playmates became almost inseparable.

NOVEMBER 1942

Growing bears are bound to get into mischief. When the 22nd Artillery Supply Company moved to a new base guarding oil fields in Iraq, Wojtek encountered something new—a clothesline of underwear dancing in the breeze.

The Women's Signals Company was not pleased!
The soldiers scolded Wojtek. He covered his eyes with his paws,
peeking out from time to time to see if the lecture was over.

JUNE 1943

Iraq's desert heat, sometimes topping 110 degrees Fahrenheit, was nearly unbearable for the soldiers, and especially for their friend in a fur coat. Wojtek sought relief in cool showers, joining the men in the bath hut each morning.

One day, soldiers found him splishing and splashing, precious water cascading over his head. Clever Wojtek had watched how the men turned on the water and used up a month's water supply!

Another night, Wojtek broke into the shower
hut, where he surprised an enemy spy hiding there.
Wojtek roared! The terrified man screamed . . .

. . . and surrendered immediately.

When questioned, the spy confessed he was a scout for raiders planning to steal Polish army intelligence and arms the following night. Fearing he would be thrown to the bear, he coughed up the names of his accomplices and they were quickly rounded up. For capturing enemy agents, Wojtek was rewarded with extra rations that night.

SEPTEMBER 1943

When the soldiers moved to another camp that fall, Wojtek was happily reunited with Kirkuk, his polka-dotted partner in crime. They resumed their games of tag, but there were dangers in the desert. "One day they picked the wrong playmate," said Henryk. "Both were [stung] by a scorpion." They bellowed in pain and became very ill. The men rushed the animals off to get help.

Wojtek's friends soon learned terrible news. Kirkuk had not survived.
Henryk stayed up with Wojtek all night, stroking his fur and
whispering softly to him.

"We thought he would die," said Dymitr.

Round-the-clock care revived their hardy bear. The next day Wojtek sat up, eyes bright, and lumbered out of bed, eager for his morning game of tag with Kirkuk. The boys' joy turned to every soldier's sorrow as they watched Wojtek search for his playmate. Henryk and Dymitr knew all too well about good friends who suddenly disappear.

Wojtek was like a brother to them now. It hurt the boys to know their beloved bear would never see his war buddy Kirkuk again.

JANUARY 1944

The months passed, and after two years of training in the Middle East, the soldiers were healthy again and battle ready. They received their marching orders and moved out to Egypt. Once there, they would board the MS *Batory*, a Polish ship bound for Italy under the British Admiralty.

There was one problem . . .

Bears were not allowed!

The rules said no pets! No mascots! After all this time, would they have to leave Wojtek behind? It was heartbreaking. Unthinkable.

Henryk and Dymitr knew the bear would never survive in the wild. He wouldn't know how to find food. Or hunt. Or defend himself. How could they abandon their best friend, their comrade, their brother? There was only one solution.

The men officially enlisted the bear as a soldier in the Polish II Corps, 22nd Artillery Supply Company. He was assigned his own paybook, rank, and serial number.

FEBRUARY 1944

When it was time, the men led the six-foot-tall bear to the gangplank.

"Private Wojtek Miś inspires fighting spirit in Polish soldiers!" cried Wojtek's friends to the astonished onlookers.

It took special approval from the high command in Cairo, but Wojtek finally led his friends onto the ship.

Once in Italy, the men got their orders: to capture Monte Cassino, an old monastery used by the Germans as an observation and artillery post. From high atop this steep, rocky hill, the Nazis blocked the Allies' route to Rome. Three other Allied armies had tried to oust the enemy—and failed. Now it was the Polish soldiers' turn.

Wojtek's company set up their supply base in a valley near Venafro. Their job was to load trucks with ammunition, food, and fuel that the drivers would deliver to the gunners in front of Monte Cassino.

General Anders rallied the troops with a reminder of what they were fighting for: their homeland. "For this action, let the lion's spirit enter your hearts," he said. "Keep deep in your heart God, honor, and our land—Poland."

MAY 11, 1944, 11 P.M.

The battle of Monte Cassino began in the dead of night and blazed for days. Round-the-clock explosions, gunfire, and smoke choked the air, the deadly sounds rebounding off the surrounding hills. At first, Wojtek climbed a tree to get a better look at the action unfolding.

"Wojtek showed he was not frightened . . . by the cannon fire,"
said Henryk. "He wanted to participate in the action."
Suddenly Henryk was called away. "It was about this time that
witnesses stated that Wojtek picked up crates full of ammunition," he said.

Legend boasts that the bear picked up live ammunition and carried it to the cannons. "That's a fairy tale," says soldier Wojciech. "He never carried bullets, let alone gave them to artillerymen." The truth was that the bear saw his friends struggling to load boxes of shells onto the trucks bound for the gunners. With the strength of four men, Wojtek lifted the crates, saving the men time and energy. More importantly, Wojtek lifted his friends' spirits. "He was a great morale boost to us all," said Henryk.

MAY 18, 1944

The fierce fighting continued for six days and six nights. The Germans fled on May 17, and the next day, the Poles joyfully raised their flag over the monastery. Their victory cleared the way for the Allies to send troops and supplies north to Rome and ultimately helped lead to the end of the war.

For his bear-hearted bravery and loyalty
to his brothers in arms, Private Wojtek
was promoted to corporal—a friend and
comrade Henryk, Dymitr, Peter, Wojciech,
and the world would never forget.

What Happened to Wojtek and His Friends?

When Irena and the Polish II Corps adopted Wojtek, they almost certainly saved him from a cruel life as a dancing bear, a form of street entertainment. At the army camp, Wojtek banded together with boys and men who truly loved him. As he grew to full size, he wore a collar and was leashed when the transport company traveled to other camps to avoid frightening other soldiers or when his friends couldn't look after him. But on the whole, the Polish soldiers treated Wojtek as a beloved brother in arms. He was critical to their recovery, both physically and emotionally. He made them laugh and love again, helping them heal from the horrors of the Siberian slave labor camps, forge bonds with each other, and later make new friends in a foreign land. When Scotland welcomed these heroes at the end of the war, Wojtek joined the parade. Decades later, the story of Wojtek continues to help veterans and their descendants open up to younger generations, and bear witness to this painful war.

> *"Wojtek the soldier bear is a powerful way to teach people about the terrible history of what the Soviet Union did and what happened to so many people like me, many of whom didn't survive the war."*
>
> —*Wojciech Narębski, last living member of Wojtek's company*

After the war, many Polish soldiers refused to return to their homeland because Stalin had installed a Soviet regime. As former prisoners of the Soviets, they knew what this murderous dictator was capable of. Britain offered a deal—the Polish Resettlement Act of 1947. It offered a new homeland to the thousands of Polish soldiers who had fought the Nazis in return for two years working in British industries like mining, forestry, or construction. Many of Wojtek's friends traveled to Scotland, where they lived in a displaced persons camp until they could settle into their new jobs, find new homes, and build new lives.

The soldiers worried about where Wojtek could live. Eventually they found him a home at the Edinburgh Zoo, where they knew he would be safe. And yet, saying goodbye was heartbreaking for bear and soldiers alike. Friends wouldn't talk about Wojtek to Peter Prendyś, because he would burst into tears at the sound of the bear's name. At the zoo, whenever Wojtek heard Polish, he would stand on his hind legs and hold up his paw. He became a popular attraction with many visitors, including Polish ex–service members, until he died in 1963, beloved by Scots and Poles alike.

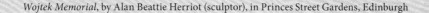

Wojtek Memorial, by Alan Beattie Herriot (sculptor), in Princes Street Gardens, Edinburgh

Bearing Arms: A Historical Note

Wojtek's role at Monte Cassino has grown legendary. One British officer claimed he witnessed Wojtek carrying actual ammunition shells to the guns. Wojciech Narębski calls that report a "fairy tale," but he confirmed that the bear helped carry boxes of shells weighing 176 to 220 pounds (80 to 100 kilograms) to load the trucks in Venafro, which the men would then deliver to the gunners firing at Monte Cassino from nearby Acquafondata.

Biologists say bears have manual dexterity and Wojtek could have hefted a crate of that weight for a short time but would not have been able to grasp a slippery single shell as often depicted. However, the 22nd Artillery Supply Company fed the legend when it changed its insignia to show Wojtek the war hero carrying a shell with a steering wheel in the background, a nod to their transport duties. The new logo appeared on company vehicles, and soldiers wore the sought-after badge on their berets and uniforms.

A badge of courage: the insignia of the 22nd Artillery Supply Company of the Polish II Corps
(Dymitr's son Andy Szawlugo)

Cub love: Irena Bokiewicz with baby Wojtek
(The Polish Institute and Sikorski Museum, London)

Coins for a cub: Polish lieutenant Anatol
Tarnowiecki purchased the bear cub for
Irena Bokiewicz. (Family archives of his
granddaughter Barbara Alicja Jańczak)

Mother Bear: The only known photo of Piotr Prendyś
(Mariusz Lukasz Zawadzki)

Brothers in arms: The smallest soldier is Wojciech
Narębski ("Little Wojtek"). (Donna Speers)

Wrestling buddies: Dymitr Szawlugo (left),
Wojtek, and Henry Zacharewicz (right)
(Dymitr's son Andy Szawlugo)

Bathtime: Cooling off in the desert heat
(The Polish Institute and Sikorski Museum, London)

Shipping out: Private Wojtek boards the MS *Batory* in Egypt.
(The Polish Institute and Sikorski Museum, London)

In the driver's seat (The Polish Institute and Sikorski Museum, London)

Brass Tacks and Bear Facts

- Anders' Army evacuated more than 74,000 Polish troops and 41,000 civilians from all over the Soviet Union, including 12,500 children under the age of fourteen. Despite some accusations of anti-Semitism, about 5,000 to 6,000 refugees were Jewish.

- Among the evacuees was Menachem Begin, later the sixth prime minister of Israel and cowinner of the Nobel Peace Prize in 1978.

- On average, brown bears weigh one pound at birth. When full-grown, Wojtek weighed almost five hundred pounds. Male bears play no part in raising cubs; the soldiers filled in as Wojtek's mother bear.

- Wojtek was not the only mascot in the Polish II Corps. Others included another bear named Michael, who attacked Wojtek and had to be given to the zoo in Tel-Aviv. In return, the zoo gave the soldiers a troublemaker and a thief—a monkey named Kasia.

- Leashes and chains were no match for clever Wojtek. If he was tethered to a stake in the ground, he would circle it, going round and round, wrapping the long chain tight until he could pull the stake up.

- When the men enlisted Wojtek, he was registered as Private Wojtek Miś (Private Wojtek Teddy Bear).

- There are war memorials to Wojtek all over the world, including Edinburgh, London, and Kraków.

September 1, 1939: Nazi Germany invades Poland from the west, starting World War II.

September 17, 1939: The Soviet Union invades Poland from the east.

September 29, 1939: Germany and the Soviet Union divide control of occupied Poland along the Bug River.

February 10, 1940: The Soviet Union begins to deport at least 1.25 million Poles to slave work camps in Siberia, according to the United States Holocaust Museum. No one knows the exact number of deportees because many were murdered in the Katyn Forest and other locations.

June 22, 1941: Nazi Germany launches a surprise attack on its ally the Soviet Union in Operation Barbarossa.

July 30, 1941: To join the Allies fighting Hitler, Stalin grudgingly frees Poles held in Siberian work camps on the condition that they fight the Nazis. General Władysław Sikorski negotiates their release in the Sikorski-Mayski Agreement.

August 17, 1941: Polish general Władysław Anders is appointed commander in chief of the Polish Army in the USSR, a.k.a. Anders' Army.

Early 1942: Wojtek is born in the Elburz Mountains in Iran (then called Persia) and orphaned by hunters. (Brown bears typically mate from May to July, with births occurring from January to March.)

March 24, 1942: The first of two evacuations of deportees leaves the USSR to cross the Caspian Sea to Pahlavi, Persia (now Bandar-e Anzali, Iran). (Second evacuation leaves August 30, 1942.)

April 8, 1942: Nineteen-year-old Irena Bokiewicz and her mother stop for the night in the Elburz Mountains on their way from Pahlavi to Tehran and meet Wojtek. Polish lieutenant Anatol Tarnowiecki purchases the bear cub from a young boy as a gift for Irena. She takes the cub with her to the civilian camp in Tehran.

August 1942: Irena donates the unnamed cub to visiting general Mieczysław Boruta-Spiechowicz, commander of the Polish 5th Infantry Division. On August 22, Lieutenant Florczykowski delivers the cub to the 2nd Transport Company of the Polish II Corps, which was later renamed the 22nd Artillery Supply Company.

April–August 1942: Anders' Army arrives in Iran. Allies push to send them into battle, but Anders insists the Polish recruits need time to recuperate from malnourishment and disease (typhus, tuberculosis, and malaria) from the gulags and to recover from the exhaustion of their long march from Siberia. Some are admitted to hospitals.

August 1942–September 1943: Anders' Army settles in Gedera, a camp in British-controlled Palestine, to train as soldiers, to practice using British weapons, and to learn English.

November 11, 1942: Wojtek and friends move to a camp in Qizil Ribat, Iraq. It's here that Wojtek swipes the clothesline of underwear belonging to the Women's Signals Company. He also breaks into the cookhouse and eats their Christmas Day dinner.

June 1943: The company moves to a camp in Kirkuk, Iraq, where Wojtek has a nasty run-in with a bear called Michael, the mascot of the 16th Lwow Rifles Battalion.

September 1943: The company continues on to Beit Jerja in Palestine. The bear Michael is given to the Tel-Aviv Zoo, which gives the company a monkey named Kasia in return.

January 17–March 15, 1944: The Allies mount three unsuccessful attempts to capture Monte Cassino.

February 14, 1944: Archibald Brown, courier to General Montgomery, registers Wojtek and his friends to board the MS *Batory*. The ship leaves Alexandria, Egypt, on February 17 and arrives in Taranto, Italy, on February 21.

May 11, 1944: Operation Diadem, the Polish assault on Monte Cassino supported by other Allied troops, begins at 11:00 p.m.

May 18, 1944: Polish troops triumphantly capture Monte Cassino, opening a road to Rome for the Allies. They paid dearly in the bloody battle, with 923 Poles dead, 2,931 injured, and 345 missing in action. Altogether, more than 55,000 Allied soldiers died in the four attempts to capture this strategic site.

June 6, 1944: D-Day; Allied troops storm the French coastline and turn the course of the war against Germany in one of the largest amphibious military assaults in history. By August, all of northern France would be liberated.

February 4–11, 1945: The Yalta Conference promises free elections in Poland, but Stalin spends the next two years installing a Communist government instead. Many Polish soldiers refuse to return to their homeland.

May 8, 1945: V-E Day, or Victory in Europe Day; the Germans surrender to the Allies on this day, ending World War II in Europe. However, the war still raged in the Pacific and the Japanese would not surrender until August 14, 1945.

September 1946: Wojtek and his friends set sail from Naples, Italy, to Glasgow, Scotland.

October 28, 1946: Wojtek and company arrive at Winfield Camp for Displaced Persons, near Hutton, Berwickshire, Scotland.

March 27, 1947: The Polish Resettlement Act offered Polish troops who had fought the Nazis an opportunity to stay in the UK permanently.

November 15, 1947: Wojtek takes up residence in the Edinburgh Zoo.

December 2, 1963: According to Edinburgh Zoo records, Wojtek dies at the age of twenty-one.

May 12, 1970: General Anders dies in London and is buried at the Polish cemetery at Monte Cassino on May 23.

1989: Poland finally gains its independence from the Soviet Union when free elections are held and citizens vote against Communism.

Maps of Wojtek's Travels

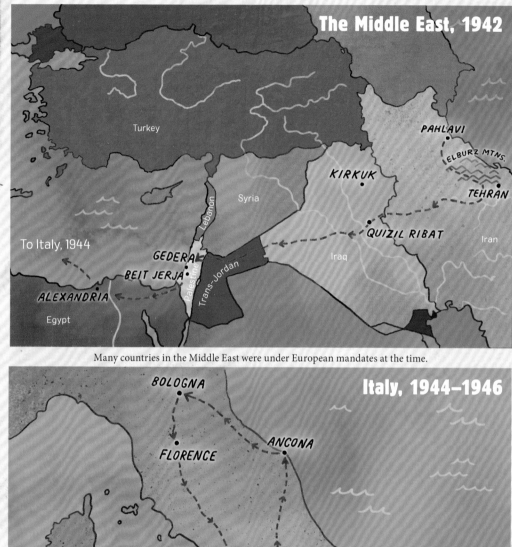

The Middle East, 1942

Turkey

PAHLAVI

ELBURZ MTNS.

KIRKUK

TEHRAN

Syria

Lebanon

QUIZIL RIBAT

Iraq

Iran

To Italy, 1944

GEDERA

BEIT JERJA

Palestine

Trans-Jordan

ALEXANDRIA

Egypt

Many countries in the Middle East were under European mandates at the time.

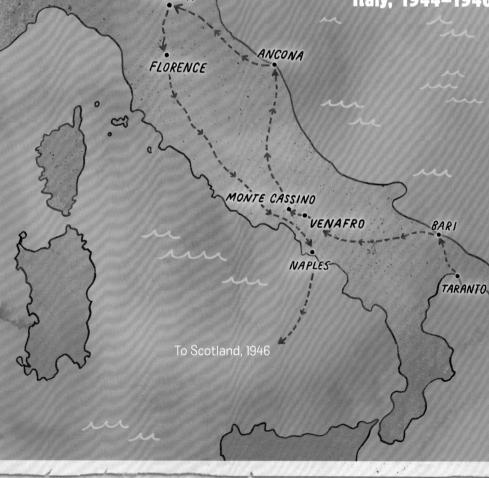

Italy, 1944–1946

BOLOGNA

ANCONA

FLORENCE

MONTE CASSINO

VENAFRO

BARI

NAPLES

TARANTO

To Scotland, 1946

Bearing Witness: Sources

Author interviews: Much has been written about Wojtek by people who care about him passionately, and many new facts have emerged in recent years. I'm indebted to the following people for sharing invaluable family memories, letters, photographs, and other documents about Wojtek and Anders' Army and for helping me try to tell the true story about this inspiring bear. Any mistakes are my own.

- Norman Davies, author of *Trail of Hope: The Anders Army, an Odyssey across Three Continents*
- Brendan Foley, writer, director, and film producer planning a movie about Wojtek
- Sonia Haynes, daughter of Henryk Zacharewicz
- Monica Helman, British Ministry of Defense
- Alan B. Herriot, sculptor of the Wojtek Memorial in Edinburgh
- Krystyna Ivell and Vic Baczor, authors of *Wojtek Album*
- Barbara Alicia Jańczak, granddaughter of Anatol Tarnowiecki
- Janek Lasocki, grandson of W. A. Lasocki (author of *Soldier Bear*)
- Aileen Orr, author of *Wojtek the Bear: Polish War Hero*
- Frank Pleszak, author of *Two Years in a Gulag*
- Agnieszka Sergiel, Polish bear biologist
- Dr. Andrzej Suchcitz, historian at the Polish Institute and Sikorski Museum

Extra special thanks to Richard Lucas, who shared many primary sources collected over the years and who put me in touch with Wojciech Narębski, who was the only surviving member of the company; to Andy Szawlugo, son of Dymitr Szawlugo, who patiently answered my endless questions; to Wojtek Deluga, film archivist at the Polish Institute and Sikorski Museum; and to Olga Kaminska, who translated many Polish documents.

Other sources include letters and documents written by Irena Bokiewicz, Wojciech Narębski, and Dymitr Szawlugo, as well as collections at the Hoover Institute, Imperial War Museum, Kresy-Siberia Foundation, and Polish Institute and Sikorski Museum.

Recommended Historical Fiction and Nonfiction

Soldier Bear, by Geoffrey Morgan and W. A. Lasocki (Collins, 1970)
Soldier Bear, by Bibi Dumon Tak, illustrated by Philip Hopman (Eerdmans, 2013)
Trail of Hope: The Anders Army, an Odyssey across Three Continents, by Norman Davies (Bloomsbury, London, 2016)
Wojtek Album, by Krystyna M. Ivell and Vic Baczor (Krystyna Ivell, 2013)
Wojtek the Bear: Polish War Hero, by Aileen Orr (Birlinn Limited, Edinburgh, 2019)

Quote Sources

Back jacket: *"We absolutely loved him"*: "Outlook—The Soldier Bear Who Went to War—BBC Sounds." BBC News. BBC. https://www.bbc.co.uk/sounds/play/p06vvk2r.

Page 12: *"The bear treated [Peter] as a father"*: Ibid.

Page 17: *"Even though he was in a bear skin"*: Ibid.

Page 25: *"One day they picked the wrong playmate."*: *Wojtek Album* by Krystyna M. Ivell and Vic Baczor, p. 59.

Page 27: *"We thought he would die"*: "The Soldier Bear" by Andres Szawlugo. http://thesoldierbear.com/dymitrszawlugo/index.html.

Page 31: *"Private Wojtek Miś inspires fighting spirit"*: "The Bear Who Helped Polish Soldiers Fight Hitler's Nazis." The Independent. Independent Digital News and Media, September 24, 2018. http://www.independent.co.uk/news/uk/home-news/wojtek-bear-named-second-world-war-film-polish-soldiers-monte-cassino-snowman-private-army-carried-a8553001.html.

Page 33: *"For this action, let the lion's spirit enter your hearts"*: "The Red Poppies of Monte Cassino" by Bogumila and Izabela Spero. *Wojtek the Bear: Polish War Hero*, by Aileen Orr, p. 46.

Page 35: *"Wojtek showed he was not frightened"*: Author interview and family documents from Sonia Haynes, daughter of Henryk Zacharewicz.

Page 36: *"That's a fairy tale"*: Document from Wojciech Narębski.

Page 36: *"He never carried bullets"*: Batalie tropiciela. http://polska-zbrojna.pl/home/articleinmagazineshow/22899?title=Batalie-tropiciela.

Page 40: *"Wojtek the soldier bear is a powerful way to teach people"*: "A Life Well Lived | Wojciech Narębski | TEDxKazimierz."

Film

Watch *Wojtek: The Bear That Went to War*. Halcyon Pictures. Vimeo, November 26, 2020.
   https://vimeo.com/ondemand/wojtek/31729119.

Websites

"Biuletyn Polonia Włoska Numer 1-2 / 2013." calaméo.com. https://en.calameo.com/read/000823018fce5ff37e1c7.

Imperial War Museums: www.iwm.org.uk.

Kresy-Siberia Virtual Museum: https://kresy-siberia.org.

Legacy.com, and Legacy. "Henryk Zacharewicz Obituary (2011)—Toronto Star." Legacy.com,
   Legacy, June 21, 2011. https://www.legacy.com/obituaries/thestar/obituary.aspx?pid=152122167.

Polish Institute and Sikorski Museum: https://pism.org.uk/.

"Comrades in Arms," The Soldier Bear. http://thesoldierbear.com/comrades/index.html.

With Gratitude

Special thanks to Bahman Azarm; my wonderful agent, Brenda Bowen; and all my good friends at HarperCollins: Nancy Inteli, Megan Ilnitzki, Chelsea C. Donaldson, Caitlin Stamper, Patty Rosati, Mimi Rankin, Kathryn Silsand, Rebecca McGuire, Seoling Dee, and Aubrey Churchward. Love and endless thanks to my husband, Paul Kueffner, and to my daughters, Emily and Allison. I couldn't do what I do without you!